SRA Open Court Reading

Genre Practice

Grade 1

Acknowledgment

"Johnny and the Toad." *Baby Chatterbox,* New York: R. Worthington, 1880.

mheducation.com/prek-12

Send all inquiries to:
McGraw-Hill Education
8787 Orion Place
Columbus, OH 43240

ISBN: 978-0-07-682455-7
MHID: 0-07-682455-1

Printed in the United States of America

2 3 4 5 6 7 8 9 10 LHS 25 24 23 22 21 20

Table of Contents

Aria's Wish

It was a horrible day! On the way to school, Aria's backpack ripped, and all her things spilled out. During lunch, she had an argument with her friend. After school, her older brother wouldn't let her play with him.

Aria marched outside and sat down on the grass. She watched a large bird flying through the sky. "I wish I had wings," said Aria. "I would fly away!"

Just then a single feather floated down. There were no other feathers in the air, just this one. Aria reached up and grabbed it. Suddenly, Aria felt a strange tingle move from her fingers, up her arm, and across her body. Long, brown feathers began to grow on Aria's arms. In seconds, Aria had grown wings in place of her arms.

Aria stood, stretched her neck, and flapped her wings. She rose from the ground. With every flap of her new wings, Aria flew higher and higher, faster and faster. Aria flew far and long before she decided to fly back to her street.

She was surprised to see her family outside, calling her name.

Aria yelled down, "Here I am!"

Her family stared at her with wide eyes as Aria landed.

"I'm so glad you're safe," Mom said as she hugged Aria. Aria tried to hug her back, but Aria's feathers tickled Mom's nose, and Mom began to sneeze.

Aria's family welcomed her into the house, but when she entered, the cat's hair stood on end.

"Coco, it's me," Aria said, but the cat just hissed louder. Aria's brother quickly let the cat outside.

Dad called the family into the kitchen for dinner. The smell of Dad's famous spaghetti made Aria's mouth water. Mom passed a plate of spaghetti to Aria, but without hands, Aria could not use her fork! Aria was so hungry, she lowered her mouth and began to eat straight from the plate. When she lifted her head, she noticed everyone was giving her a strange look. It made Aria feel terrible.

Aria ran outside and flew off into the air. "I don't want wings," she sobbed. "I wish I had my arms back!" As she said this, her feathers fell off, one by one. Aria slowly drifted down and landed in her yard.

Her family gathered around. "You're back!" they said.

Aria hugged them tightly, "Yes, and I want to stay here, even on my worst days!"

Respond to Reading

1. yes   no

2.

3. yes   no

4.

What is the first thing that happens after Aria grows wings?

Aria _____ in the air.

Fantasy • *Genre Practice*

Fun in the Rain

When it rains, you can feel stuck inside the house. But don't let a rainy day keep you indoors every time. Just put on your boots and raincoat, and then head outside to play! You might have a better time than you ever imagined. There are surprising ways to enjoy even the wettest days. Get your parents' permission, and head outside in the rain to find some fun.

The best part about rainy days is playing in puddles! If you're wearing rain boots, you can jump in puddles. Watch how far you can send the water flying! How many splashes does it take to empty a puddle?

You can even float boats in puddles. Try floating different kinds of small boats, like ones made from wood, folded paper, or plastic. Figure out which kind floats the best and is the most fun to play with. If your boat has a sail, try making your own wind to send the boat across the water. Maybe you can have a boat race with your friends!

Wet days are also a great time to play in the mud. You can cover your hands in mud and squeeze it between your fingers or kick off your shoes and socks and squish the mud between your toes. What are the different sounds that mud can make?

You can also mix dirt and water to make mud. Then you can form and shape the mud like dough. Later, you can see how long the shapes last. You can even draw or write on the ground. You can use sticks to draw in smooth mud or wet sand. You can send messages to your friends by writing in the wet ground.

On rainy days, you can explore how water affects the land in your neighborhood. See if the rain made new streams or waterfalls. You can count how long it takes rain water to run down a hill or a street.

You can even measure the rain! Collect the rain water in a bucket, and use your ruler to measure how many inches of rain fell. Keep track of the amounts each time it rains. Can you find a pattern in the numbers?

Playing outdoors in the rain is more fun than you might think. So don't let rainy weather ruin your day! Head outside, and have a great time, even when the sky is gloomy and gray.

Persuasive Text • *Genre Practice*

Respond to Reading

1. yes   no

2.

3.

4. yes   no

Why does the author want children to play in the rain?

Playing in the rain is _____.

Turning Dirt into Gold

Long ago, a young woman and a young man fell in love. Soon, they were married. The young woman was mostly happy, but her new husband refused to get a job.

"I work hard to earn money," she said. "But what do you do?"

"I am an alchemist," her husband said. "I can turn dirt into gold. I haven't done it yet, but soon I'll be able to make lots of gold!"

Time passed, however, and the young alchemist did not make any gold. The young woman told her father about her husband's struggle. Her father agreed to talk to her husband.

The young alchemist explained his work to his father-in-law. The older man nodded and said, "I, too, was an alchemist when I was young. You can turn dirt into gold, but you are missing something important."

The young alchemist begged his father-in-law for advice, and the older man explained, "You must collect two pounds of silver powder, which can only be found on the leaves of banana trees."

The young alchemist exclaimed, "I'll have to plant hundreds of banana trees to get that much silver!"

"That's true," replied his father-in-law. "But if you are willing to work hard, I will buy the land for your trees."

The young alchemist worked hard, planting hundreds of banana trees and taking care of them. The young woman sold the bananas at the market, while the alchemist carefully collected silver powder from each leaf. It took many years to collect what he needed.

Finally, he had enough silver. He took it to his father-in-law, who smiled and said, "Now we will need my daughter's help."

They went back to the young couple's house and the older man asked his daughter, "What did you do with all the bananas that grew here?"

"I sold them at the market, of course," she replied.

"Did you save any of the money?" the father asked.

The young woman nodded and showed two large bags of gold coins. Her husband was amazed.

"You planted and cared for the banana trees," the older man said to the alchemist. "And you sold the fruit," he said to his daughter. "Together, you turned dirt into gold!"

A smile spread across the young man's face because he understood the lesson: hard work results in gold. "You are the wisest alchemist," he told his father-in-law. "Thank you for sharing your wisdom."

Folktale • *Genre Practice*

Respond to Reading

1. yes   no

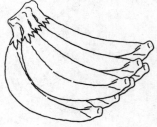  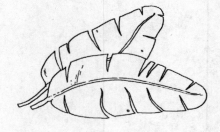

2.

3. yes   no

4.

Why does the young man work hard on the land?

He works hard to turn _____ into gold.

Henry Bergh: A Hero to Animals

Do you love animals? Henry Bergh sure did! He helped improve the lives of millions of animals.

Henry Bergh was born in New York City in the year 1813. After Henry's father died, Henry inherited a lot of money. So Henry and his wife decided to travel the world. One day, Henry was in a city in Russia. Back then, people in cities used horses to get around instead of cars and trains. Henry saw a man being mean and cruel to a horse because the horse had fallen in the street.

Henry Bergh was very upset when he saw the horse being treated badly. He thought about his hometown of New York City. He realized that many horses in New York City might also be treated poorly. Henry didn't want people to hurt animals at all, so he decided to do something to put a stop to it.

Henry started talking to his friends about the unfair way animals were often treated. Henry's friends listened to him, and many of them agreed with his ideas. Many of these friends were powerful politicians. They could make laws that would help protect animals from harm.

In 1866, Henry started the American Society for the Prevention of Cruelty to Animals, or the ASPCA. Soon after, politicians in New York passed a law that said people could not be cruel to animals. The ASPCA was then able to arrest people that broke the law. Henry became president of the ASPCA. He spent a lot of time on the streets of New York City. He looked for people being cruel to animals. If he saw people breaking the law, Henry arrested them.

Henry worked hard to stop humans from mistreating animals. He believed animals had the right to be treated with respect and kindness. Because of his work, ASPCA groups started in other cities. Soon, other states adopted animal protection laws like the ones in New York.

Henry Bergh died in 1888, but he is still remembered today as a hero for helping protect animals.

Respond to Reading

1. yes   no

2.

3. yes   no

4.

What did Henry do as president of the ASPCA?

Henry made sure people treated _____ with kindness.

Biography • *Genre Practice*

Take Care of Your Pet

Do you or any of your friends have a pet? Pets can be great friends, but it is a lot of work to take care of them! Pets need food, water, and exercise. They need a clean and comfortable place to live. It is also important to remember that not all animals are alike. Different kinds of pets need different kinds of care.

Have you ever seen a pet fish swimming around in a tank? If you decide to own a fish, put a filter in the tank to keep the water fresh. Otherwise, the fish's water will get dirty and cloudy. Put some rocks and plants in the tank so your fish can play around them. Your fish might like a small place to hide when it's feeling shy! To feed your fish, sprinkle fish food on top of the water, and watch your fish eat!

Have you ever petted a gerbil? Gerbils are fluffy, cute little animals. Gerbils need a safe place to live. Lay down some soft bedding in a cage or an aquarium. Gerbils eat pet food, but you can also feed them bits of apple or lettuce as a treat. A pet gerbil might tip over its water bowl, so get a special upside-down water bottle to hang on the side of the cage. Gerbils love to explore outside their cage, but make sure your gerbil does not get lost!

Dogs make great pets, but they need plenty of exercise. Take your dog walking or running at least once a day. Dogs love to play fetch with balls or sticks, and they love to be petted and scratched. Be sure to give your dog plenty of fresh water, too, because dogs can get very thirsty. It's also important to feed your dog the right amount of food so it can stay healthy.

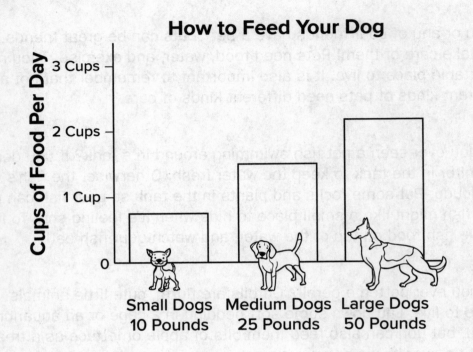

How to Feed Your Dog

Owning pets is a joyful experience, but it's also a big responsibility. Make sure your pet has food and water, a safe place to live, and the right kind of exercise and activities. Take good care of your pet. Your animal friend is counting on you!

Respond to Reading

1. yes   no

2.

3.

4. yes   no

What do we need to give our pets?

Pets need water, a safe home, and good _____ to eat.

Informational Text • *Genre Practice*

Ant and Grasshopper

One summer day, under the shade of a big oak tree, Grasshopper was playing his fiddle. As he played, he danced merrily. When Ant marched by carrying a piece of grain on her back, Grasshopper invited her to join him. "Come and dance to my music, Ant!"

Without stopping, Ant replied, "I'm busy gathering food to store for the cold winter, Grasshopper, and you should do the same."

Grasshopper chuckled, "You worry too much. There is plenty of time to gather food for the winter. For now, I will play music and dance."

Several weeks passed, and there was a chill in the air. Wearing a jacket, Grasshopper tucked the fiddle under his chin and began to play while he stomped on the fallen leaves.

Once again, Ant passed by carrying grain. "Ant, my friend," Grasshopper said, "put that grain down and stomp on the leaves while I play. We can make great songs together!"

Ant answered in a frustrated voice, "I must collect food! Winter will soon be here."

Grasshopper laughed, "You worry too much, Ant! There is plenty of time to gather food for the winter, but right now I'm making music!"

As the weeks passed, the days grew colder and shorter, and still Grasshopper played his fiddle. He often saw Ant and invited her to join in his fun, but she always refused and warned Grasshopper about the coming winter.

One morning, Grasshopper was surprised to find a blanket of snow covering the ground. He tucked his fiddle under his chin and began to play, but soon he started shivering, and his stomach growled. Grasshopper decided to search for some food. He looked and looked, but the plants were all covered in snow. Grasshopper became worried. What would he eat?

Grasshopper remembered all the times he saw Ant carrying grain on her back to store for the winter. He went to her house to ask for food. By the time Grasshopper arrived, he was shaking and weak from cold and hunger.

Ant opened the door and gasped at the sight of Grasshopper. When Grasshopper asked if he could eat some of her food, Ant shook her head and exclaimed, "I warned you, Grasshopper!"

Grasshopper lowered his head and turned to walk away. "Wait," Ant called, "I cannot let you go hungry. I will share, but only a little and only this year."

Grasshopper hugged Ant and said, "Oh, Ant, thank you! I understand now. There is a time for work and a time for play."

Respond to Reading

1. yes   no

2.

3.

4. yes   no

What is Grasshopper's biggest problem in the story?

Grasshopper is hungry because he _____ all summer and fall.

The Princess and the Pea

Once upon a time, a lonely prince named Alvin traveled all over the world to search for a real princess to marry. Many women he met claimed to be princesses, but they could not prove that they were true royalty. He simply could not find a true princess to marry, so he journeyed sadly back to his castle, alone.

On the night of Prince Alvin's return, a terrible storm burst upon the kingdom. The wind howled, rain poured from the sky, lightning flashed, and thunder boomed. All in all, it was a terrible night to be outside. Suddenly, there was a knock at the castle door. When the guards opened the large wooden door, there stood a girl, soaking wet. The poor girl was a sight to be seen. Water dripped from her hair and her clothing. Her shoes squished on the cold stone floor of the castle. She left wet footprints as she padded inside.

One guard asked the girl for her name, and she replied, "I am Princess Alia." The guards gave each other a questioning look, and the one who had not yet spoken left to inform the queen. When the queen came down to meet Princess Alia she was shocked. How could this wretched, poorly dressed girl be a princess? Was it even possible?

The queen thought, "Ah, I know how to test her to see whether she is truly a princess!" She invited Alia to stay the night at the castle. While her attendants prepared the guest room, the queen secretly placed a single pea under the mattress of the bed. Then she told her attendants to pile twenty mattresses and twenty down comforters on top. "We shall see if she is truly a princess as she says," thought the queen. She showed Alia to the room and wished her a good night.

The next morning at breakfast, Alvin and Alia talked and laughed about the big storm. The queen leaned over and asked her guest how she had slept. "Oh, I had a dreadful night! I slept very poorly!" exclaimed Alia. "I do not know what could have been under that bed, but there was a lump that kept me awake for most of the night."

The queen clapped her hands with joy. At last, here was a real princess fit for her son. The girl was so sensitive and delicate that she had felt the small pea beneath the pile of mattresses and comforters. Prince Alvin and Princess Alia married later on, and everyone lived happily ever after.

Fairy Tale • *Genre Practice*

Respond to Reading

1. yes   no

2.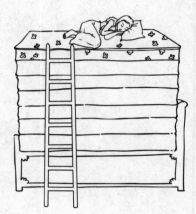

3.

4. yes   no

How does everyone feel at the end of the story?

Everyone feels _____ at the end of the story.

Fairy Tale • *Genre Practice*

Benjamin Franklin

Benjamin Franklin was born in Boston in January 1706. He grew up to become a famous American. As an adult, he was a scientist, an inventor, and a politician, but his love of learning began when he was very young.

Young Ben loved to read and write. Ben's older brother was a newspaper printer, and Ben wrote articles for the newspaper when he was only a teenager. Later, Ben opened his own printing shop in Philadelphia. Ben made a book once each year called *Poor Richard's Almanack.* It was full of wise sayings.

Ben started public programs in Philadelphia to improve the lives of others. He started the first library and the city's first fire and police departments. He also helped start a hospital and a college.

Ben was interested in science, especially electricity. He flew a kite in an experiment to prove electricity and lightning were the same thing. This led to the invention of the lightning rod. Lightning rods protect people's homes from fire during a lightning storm.

Ben was one of the country's founders. His signature is on many important documents, including the Declaration of Independence and the United States Constitution. Ben Franklin died in 1790. He was 84 years old.

Fly a Kite!

CHARACTERS

BEN

MARY, a neighbor

WILLIAM, Ben's son

(Ben Franklin flies a kite during a lightning storm in Philadelphia in 1752. Mary approaches him.)

MARY: Hello, neighbor!

BEN: Oh, hello, Mary!

MARY: What are you doing out here in this storm?

BEN: Flying a kite, of course!

MARY: Why on Earth would you fly a kite in a lightning storm? Why not wait for a sunny day?

BEN: I want to prove that lightning contains electricity. I put a metal key on this kite, and the key is connected to this jar. *(Ben shows Mary the jar attached to the kite string.)*

MARY: But Ben, I think you might get hurt doing this experiment!

BEN: Don't worry, Mary, I won't touch the key. We only need to see if this jar picks up an electrical charge in the storm. If I'm right, we can figure out a way to keep houses safe in lightning storms. *(Ben's son William comes out to the yard, noticing the weather.)*

WILLIAM: Hi, Dad! Hi, Mary! What are you two doing out here in this terrible storm? *(Ben and Mary look at each other and smile. Mary turns to William.)*

MARY: We're conducting an experiment!

Respond to Reading

1. biography   fantasy

2. yes   no

3. folktale   play

4. yes   no

What is something Ben does in both selections?

Ben flies a _____ in both selections.

Comparing Genres • *Genre Practice*

Snowflakes

Have you ever looked closely at a snowflake? It is sparkly and white. If you look even closer, you can see dazzling details. Nearly all snowflakes are different, but they are also alike in many ways. Let's find out about how snowflakes are made!

Snowflakes are a special kind of frozen water. Snowflakes form when water vapor freezes. Water vapor is like fog, except high up in the clouds instead of on the ground. When the water vapor inside a cloud freezes, it turns into tiny bits of icy dust that grow into snowflakes. The snowflakes fall when they get too heavy to stay in the cloud. As they drift down toward the ground, they gather more moisture. They keep growing until they fall to the ground as beautifully shaped snowflakes.

Most snowflakes have six sides, or "arms." When the air temperature is just below freezing, the water vapor forms crystals, each with six arms growing from it. Then, icy branches grow from these arms. As the air gets colder, the snowflakes become flatter as they freeze. This means that different temperatures can make different snowflake shapes.

The snowflakes fall through different layers of air as they come down. Each layer has a different temperature and amount of water. These changing conditions affect the way each snowflake grows. Because each snowflake takes a different path from the cloud to the ground, each snowflake grows differently. If you compare snowflakes under a magnifying glass, you will see many different shapes, sizes, and designs. It is very rare to find two snowflakes that are exactly alike.

Scientists group snowflakes by their shape and size. First, they look at the shape of the crystal at the center of the snowflake. Then, they look at the shape of the arms and smaller branches. The branches can look like needles or plates.

Sometimes the wind can change the shape of snowflakes before they hit the ground. Sometimes snowflakes can stick together in clusters. But no matter how they form, each snowflake adds to the beauty of a snowy day.

Respond to Reading

1. yes   no

2.

3.   4   5   6

4. yes   no

How is each snowflake different?

Each snowflake has a different _____ and size.

A New Home

There once was a family of mice who lived in a hole, in the wall of an apartment, on the top floor of a tall building in New York City. Mama, Papa, and the two children, Carl and Phoebe, often sat in front of their window and looked out across the river. There, they could see a giant lady with a crown and torch that lived on a small island.

One day, while the mouse family was gathering crumbs from the kitchen, a piece of paper slid under the front door. Papa Mouse unfolded the paper and read aloud. "As you know, the building will be demolished in two weeks. Please make your final arrangements to be moved out of the building by Friday."

"Oh no!" Mama Mouse exclaimed. "The building is being destroyed! We have to move out quickly!"

Phoebe asked in a panic, "Where will we go? What will we do?"

Carl looked out the window and said, "Let's go to the tall lady's island!"

Papa replied, "That's a great idea, Carl. I heard the human family say her name is Lady Liberty and that she welcomes everyone who comes to her!"

The family gathered all their belongings. Soon, they made their way out of the building and down to the water's edge. They saw a large boat filling up with people, and they carefully snuck on board.

As the boat arrived, the family could see a sign that read "Statue of Liberty." Everyone in the family looked up—way, way up. Phoebe twitched her nose and said, "The sign says Lady Liberty is a statue. I don't think she's a real human after all."

Carl pointed at an opening near the lady's feet and exclaimed, "Look! People are going inside!"

The mice followed the crowd. Once inside, they found a winding staircase. Slowly and steadily, the mice climbed to the top. Finally, they came to a set of windows. They looked out and were amazed by the view in front of them.

"I can see our old building across the water!" cried Phoebe.

Mama and Papa decided the beautiful statue of Lady Liberty would be the family's new home.

"There is a lot of space to run and play," they told the children. "There's also plenty to eat from all the people who visit every day."

Carl smiled and said, "Thank you, Lady Liberty, for the warm welcome home!"

Respond to Reading

1. yes   no

2.

3.

4. yes   no

Why does the family find a new place to live?

The building the family lives in is going to be _____ .

Let Kids Help!

When grownups in the community decide to build a new playground, children should help design it. After all, it is made for the kids! If children help plan the playground, they will feel a sense of ownership. They will feel the playground belongs to them. That means they will want to take good care of their playground. Best of all, children will learn important skills when they work on a big project with adults. Children will learn about teamwork and cooperation. Having them help with the playground project will be good for the whole community.

Children should have a chance to talk about what they want to have on their playground. Maybe some kids will want a slide and monkey bars. Maybe some will want swings. If we do not know what the children want on the playground, they may not use the playground when it is built. What kind of things would you want on a playground that is built in your neighborhood?

Most people take good care of things they have helped create. Letting children help design the playground will encourage them to take better care of it. The children will be more likely to use the equipment correctly. They will want to keep the playground clean. It will seem like it belongs to them. The children will take pride in the work they did to help design the playground.

Finally, think about the many lessons and skills that the children will be learning. These lessons and skills will be important for the children as they grow up. Kids of all ages will benefit from being on a team and from helping to make big decisions.

Adults will also be able to share their opinions about what should and should not be a part of the playground. Playgrounds have to be safe, and every part of the playground costs money. Adults can help the children understand why certain choices might be better.

Please allow children to help design their community playground. They can help pick out fun equipment that all children will enjoy. They will experience a sense of ownership and take good care of the new playground. They will also learn many important lessons and skills for later in life. Their work on the playground will benefit the community in many ways for years to come.

Respond to Reading

1. yes   no

2.

3.

4. yes   no

Why did the author write about children designing playgrounds?

The author believes adults should _____ to children's ideas.

Persuasive Text • *Genre Practice*

Grasshopper and Toad

Long ago, Grasshopper and Toad were great friends. One day, Toad invited Grasshopper to his house for dinner. "I will cook a feast for you tonight," Toad said.

"Thank you very much, Toad," replied Grasshopper. "I'll see you tonight!"

That evening, when Grasshopper arrived at Toad's house, Toad welcomed him inside. "The food smells wonderful," Grasshopper said excitedly. The two friends had never had dinner together before. They were happy to spend more time with each other.

"Our meal is ready," said Toad. "But let's wash up before we begin." Grasshopper followed Toad to the water bowl where the two friends began to wash up. As Grasshopper rubbed his forelegs together in the water, they made a loud chirping noise. It surprised Toad, but he kept quiet.

The two friends then sat at Toad's table and began to eat. As Grasshopper used his knife and fork, his forelegs rubbed together, and the chirping started again. Toad dropped his fork, surprised again.

"Please, Grasshopper," said Toad, sounding a little annoyed, "I cannot enjoy my meal with you chirping like that. Keep it down!"

"I'm sorry, Toad," replied Grasshopper. He was embarrassed, but he was not able to stop the chirping. Each time Grasshopper made the noise, Toad glared at him before taking another bite. Eventually, Grasshopper said, "Excuse me," and rose from the table to leave.

The next evening, Grasshopper invited Toad to come eat dinner at Grasshopper's house. When Toad arrived, Grasshopper explained dinner was almost ready. Then he said, "Before we eat, we should wash up." Toad hopped after Grasshopper to the water bowl. Grasshopper chirped as he washed, and Toad frowned. Toad quickly rinsed his hands and then followed Grasshopper to the table. As Toad hopped along the dirt floor, dirt stuck to his legs. Grasshopper noticed the dirt and said sternly, "You cannot sit at my table with dirt on you! Go wash again."

Toad hopped back to the water bowl and rewashed, but when he hopped back to the table, of course the dirt stuck to his wet skin again. Grasshopper still would not let Toad sit at the table.

"You know I can't stop dirt from sticking to my skin!" Toad yelled.

"As a matter of fact, I do," said Grasshopper. "Just as *you* know I cannot stop chirping when I rub my legs together!"

Toad stormed out of Grasshopper's house. It was sad, because Toad and Grasshopper could be friends if only each would accept what the other was not able to change.

Respond to Reading

1. yes   no

2.

3.

4. yes   no

What should Grasshopper accept about Toad?

Grasshopper should accept that _____ sticks
to Toad's feet.

Bill Melendez: Bringing Drawings to Life

Do you like Mickey Mouse? Have you ever seen Daffy Duck or Bugs Bunny in a cartoon? Maybe you have laughed at Snoopy in a Charlie Brown movie. If so, then you have seen the work of Bill Melendez.

Bill was born in Mexico in 1916. His parents gave him the name José Cuauhtémoc Melendez. Young José loved to draw. He drew pictures of the many things he saw in Mexico. When he was about twelve, his family moved to the United States. José continued to draw.

When he was in his early twenties, José showed his drawings to people at the Walt Disney company. They liked his pictures and hired him as an animator. An animator makes a series of drawings, called frames. When the frames are shown one after another, very quickly, the characters in the drawings look like they are moving. These frames become the animated movies you watch. José helped animate movies like *Pinocchio* and *Bambi*. José also animated cartoons featuring Mickey Mouse and Donald Duck. Because the name "José Cuauhtémoc Melendez" was so long, the credits at the end of the movies listed his name as "Bill Melendez."

Do you recognize the name Charlie Brown? A man named Charles Schulz created Charlie Brown and his friends and called them "the Peanuts." When Bill was in his late forties, he worked with Schulz to animate the Peanuts in a television special called *A Charlie Brown Christmas*. Bill also played the voice of Snoopy in the movie. If you have seen a Charlie Brown movie, you know Snoopy, the dog, doesn't talk. So Bill recorded himself saying nonsense words. He sped up the tape and used it for Snoopy's voice. Bill won an important award for his work on the show, and he went on to win even more!

In the 1960s, Bill Melendez opened his own studio where he made commercials, television shows, and films. You may recognize the name Garfield—a big, orange cat drawn by Jim Davis. Bill's studio brought Garfield to life through animation.

Bill died in 2008 at the age of 91. But Bill's son, Steven, helps run the studio now. People at the studio continue to work on commercials, television shows, and movies, bringing characters like the Peanuts to life through animation!

Respond to Reading

1. yes   no

2.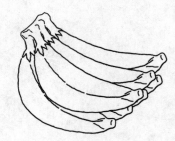

3.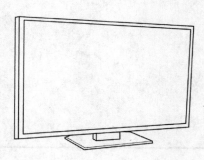

4. yes   no

What was Bill's job?

Bill made illustrations look like they were _____.

Aloha, Alex!

October 23

Aloha, Alex!

I just love being in Hawaii! I should probably explain my greeting, though. Hawaiian words are very different from the words we use every day, but to me they sound musical. "Aloha" means "hello" in Hawaiian. Aloha from Hawaii!

Hawaii is made up of many small islands that are clustered together in the middle of the Pacific Ocean. I'm staying on Oahu, one of the bigger islands. Honolulu is the capital city of Hawaii, and it's here on Oahu. It's a big American city, and it looks a lot like other cities in America.

The beaches here are fantastic! The sand is so soft under your feet. The weather in Hawaii is tropical, which means that it is warm almost all year round. Because of the constant warmth, the ocean water is the perfect temperature for swimming. I've been snorkeling a few times already, and we saw lots of fish and coral! But I have to tell you about more than just the beaches. There are incredible mountains here, too, and even active volcanoes!

On some of the Hawaiian Islands, people can walk right up to the edge of a volcano. You can look down into the molten lava! To visit the other Hawaiian Islands, people take a plane or a boat. I flew to Kauai last week, which is a smaller island with beautiful rain forests. I learned a lot about the different plants here in Hawaii. There are lovely orchids, which are unusual flowers—very large and colorful.

I hiked to a huge waterfall when I was in Kauai. I saw farmers growing macadamia nuts on the steep hillsides. I even got to tour the plant where workers package the macadamia nuts to send to the rest of the United States (which islanders call the "mainland"). I know you really like the macadamia nuts your mom buys at the store. I picked up some nuts for your family, and I'll bring them to you next time I see you!

Well, it's nearly time for my surfing lesson, so I'll finish this letter. Let me teach you one more interesting fact about the Hawaiian language before I go. In Hawaii, people can use exactly the same word to say "good-bye" as they use to say "hello!" So, aloha, Alex! I'll see you when I get back to the mainland!

Love,

Aunt Jill

Respond to Reading

1. yes   no

2.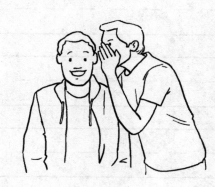

3.

4. yes   no

Mountains!

In places all around the world, mountains rise into the sky. Mountains are beautiful and can be fun places to explore! The United States has lots of mountains and mountain ranges. A mountain range is a collection of mountains all strung together across the land. Let's learn about the two biggest mountain ranges in the United States and why people love living near mountains. Climb up to the top, and take a look!

The Appalachian Mountains stretch from Canada in the North all the way down to Alabama in the South. The Appalachians are extremely old. When people first arrived in North American, the mountains were here to greet them. Over time, the weather and seasons have eroded the Appalachian Mountains. So today, they are smaller and have many more trees than younger mountains. People do a lot of hiking in the Appalachians!

The Rocky Mountains are a mountain range in the western United States. The Rockies are much, much taller than the Appalachians. The Rockies are also not as old as the Appalachians. The peaks of the Rocky Mountains are sharper and more jagged, too, and with fewer trees. This is because the weather has had a lot less time to erode the Rockies' sharp edges. But it also means the Rockies are perfect for skiing!

There are many reasons people love to be near mountains. For one, the views are spectacular! There are also mountain parks with hiking, camping, and nature tours. Lucky visitors may see unusual wildlife on their hikes. In the Rocky Mountains, you might see elk, big horn sheep, and mountain goats. In the Appalachian Mountains you can see white-tailed deer, moose, and beavers. So if you ever have the chance, go and visit a mountain. You'll see that mountains are fun places to climb, hike, and explore—or just sit and enjoy the view!

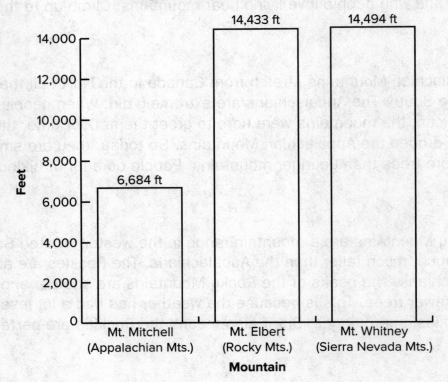

Informational Text • *Genre Practice*

Respond to Reading

1. yes   no

2.

3.

4. yes   no

Why do mountains erode over time?

Mountains erode over time because of _____

and seasons.

Johnny and the Toad

JOHNNY.

I want to go to school,

   And he won't let me pass.

I think that a toad

   OUGHT to keep to the grass.

I don't want to cry,

   But I'm afraid I'm going to;

Oh, dear me!

   What am I to do?

TOAD.

Here's a dreadful thing!

   A boy in the way;

I don't know what to do,

   I don't know what to say.

I can't see the reason

   Such monsters should be loose;

I'm trembling all over,

   But that is of no use.

JOHNNY.

I MUST go to school,
    The bell is going to stop;
That terrible old toad,
    If only he would hop.

TOAD.

I MUST cross the path,
    I can hear my children croak;
I hope that dreadful boy
    Will not give me a poke.

A hop, and a start, a flutter, and a rush,
Johnny is at school, and the toad is in his bush.

Respond to Reading

1. yes   no

2.

3.

4. yes   no

Why does the toad want to get across the path?

The toad's _____ are on the other side of

the path.

Name _____ Date _____

Lemonade vs. Popcorn

Characters

TIMOTHY, JAN'S best friend

JAN, TIMOTHY'S best friend

(A quiet neighborhood on a warm summer afternoon. Timothy and Jan are sitting on the front steps of Timothy's house.)

TIMOTHY: I have a great idea, Jan! Let's set up a stand and sell snacks to the people in the neighborhood.

JAN: I could definitely use some money.

TIMOTHY: (*shading his eyes against the sun*) We could put our table over there.

JAN: Good idea! I'll head inside and get Mom to help me make some popcorn. Then we could put it in little bags to sell for fifty cents.

TIMOTHY: (*annoyed*) Popcorn? No, that's a terrible idea! People will want lemonade because it's so hot out.

JAN: But popcorn is a nutritious, healthy snack. I know people won't want all that sugary lemonade!

TIMOTHY: Lemonade will help people cool down, so we're selling lemonade.

JAN: (*angrily*) Maybe YOU are selling lemonade, but MY stand will sell popcorn, and that's final!

(The two children stomp off in different directions.)

(*Later in the afternoon, Jan sets up a table to sell popcorn. Timothy sets up a table to sell lemonade. The children can see each other, but they are too angry to speak. A man visits Jan's popcorn table.*)

JAN: (*to the man*) Thank you, and send your friends by for more popcorn!

(*The man leaves the stage.*)

JAN: (*talking to herself*) Whew, it's so hot out here that I wish I had a cool drink!

(*A woman approaches Timothy's table and purchases lemonade.*)

TIMOTHY: Thank you, and I hope you enjoy that nice, cool lemonade!

(*The woman leaves the stage.*)

TIMOTHY: Gosh, I must be getting hungry! Popcorn sure sounds delicious right now. Maybe Jan will share. (*yelling*) Hey, Jan! Do you want some lemonade? I have extra.

JAN: (*yelling*) Lemonade sounds great, Timothy, and I could share some popcorn.

(*The two children meet between their tables, bringing lemonade and popcorn.*)

JAN: Thank you. This tastes delicious!

TIMOTHY: Thank YOU. The popcorn is really good. I was hungry. Hey, I have another wonderful idea. Let's put our tables together and sell both popcorn AND lemonade.

JAN: I think that would be great. I bet even more people will come if we have both things together, so let's do it!

(*Timothy and Jan move their tables next to each other, and then several people stop to buy snacks. The children smile at each other.*)

Play • *Genre Practice*

Respond to Reading

1. yes   no

2.

3.

4. yes   no

How do people feel when they solve a problem together?

Solving a problem together makes people feel _____.

Name _____ Date _____

The Two Goats

Read the passage below. Then answer the questions that follow.

Once, there were two mountains. A river ran between them. There was a bridge over the river. It went from one mountain to the other.

One day, two goats stepped onto the bridge. One goat was on one side. The other goat was on the other side. Both goats began to cross. They met in the middle. The bridge was wide enough for only one goat to pass.

The first goat said, "Go back! I want to cross!"

The second goat said, "You go back! I want to cross!"

The goats did not move. Then they lowered their heads. They charged at each other. The goats hit their horns together very hard. They both fell off! Splash! Splash! They landed in the river below.

Each goat climbed out of the river. Again, they climbed to the bridge. And again they met each other in the middle.

One goat lowered his head. He was ready to fight again!
But the other goat said, "Wait! If we fight, we are sure to
fall off. I have an idea. I will lie down. You can climb over me.
Then we can both get to the other side."

"OK, let's do it," said the other goat.

They put the plan into action. One goat climbed over the
other. It worked!

"Working together is better than fighting," said one goat.

"I agree," said the other goat. And both goats went their
own ways.

Name _____ **Date** _____

Respond to Reading

Read each question. Circle the letter next to your answer choice.

1. This passage—

   a. is a fable.

   b. is a play.

   c. is a biography.

2. Why did the author most likely write the passage?

   a. to tell a sad story

   b. to give information

   c. to teach a lesson

3. Which is the BEST summary of the passage?

   a. One goat wants to eat new plants. Another goat wants to see a new place. The goats cross a path.

   b. Two goats meet on a bridge. At first they fight and fall into the river. Then they work together to cross.

   c. A bridge connects two mountains. There is a river down below. Only one goat can cross.

REREAD "The Two Goats" on pages 73–74.

THINK about how the author describes what the goats do. Why do the goats fight? Use the Five Ws Chart on page 149 to organize your ideas.

What does the author want the reader to learn? Use details from the story to support your answer.

_____

_____

_____

_____

_____

_____

_____

Be sure to—

1. answer the question, "What does the author want the reader to learn?"

2. use details from the passage to support your answer.

3. use your own words.

Goldilocks and the Three Bears

Read the passage below. Then answer the questions that follow.

Once upon a time, three bears made soup for dinner. The soup needed to cool. So the bears went for a walk.

A little girl went in their house. Her name was Goldilocks. She was hungry. She tasted the soup. Papa Bear's soup was too hot. Mama Bear's soup was too cold. Baby Bear's soup was just right. She ate all of Baby Bear's soup.

Goldilocks felt tired. She saw three chairs. One chair was too hard. The next chair was too soft. The little chair was just right. Goldilocks sat on it. The chair broke!

Goldilocks felt sleepy. She went to lie down. Papa Bear's bed was too hard. Mama Bear's bed was too soft. Baby Bear's bed was just right. Goldilocks fell asleep.

Then the bears came home.

"Someone's been eating my soup!" said Papa Bear.

"Someone's been eating my soup!" said Mama Bear.

"Someone's been eating my soup!" said Baby Bear. "It's all gone!"

The bears went into the next room.

"Someone's been sitting in my chair," said Papa Bear.

"Someone's been sitting in my chair," said Mama Bear.

"Someone's been sitting in my chair!" said Baby Bear. "It's broken!"

The bears went to the bedroom.

"Someone's been sleeping in my bed," said Papa Bear.

"Someone's been sleeping in my bed," said Mama Bear.

"Someone IS sleeping in my bed!" cried Baby Bear.

Goldilocks woke up. She was scared! Goldilocks ran away. She never went back to the Bears' house.

Name _____ **Date** _____

Respond to Reading

Read each question. Circle the letter next to your answer choice.

1. This passage—

   a. gives information.

   b. is a fairy tale.

   c. is a poem.

2. Why was Baby Bear's bed best for Goldilocks?

   a. It was just right.

   b. It was big.

   c. It was very soft.

3. What lesson does this story teach?

   a. You should not go for walks in the woods.

   b. You should not eat soup that is too cold.

   c. You should not use what is not yours.

REREAD "Goldilocks and the Three Bears" on pages 77–78.

THINK about things that help you know this story is a fairy tale. What parts of the story show that it is a fairy tale? Use the Word Map on page 150 to organize your ideas.

How can you tell this story is a fairy tale? Write two details from this story that show that the story is a fairy tale.

_____
– –
_____
– –
_____
– –
_____
– –
_____
– –

Be sure to—

1. include details that show this story is a fairy tale.

2. use correct spelling.

3. use a capital letter at the start of every sentence.

4. use an end mark at the end of every sentence.

A Tale of the Wind and the Sun

Read the passages below. Then answer the questions that follow.

Wind and Sun were arguing about who was stronger. They looked down from the sky and saw a man walking.

Sun said, "Whoever can make that man take off his coat first wins."

Wind went first. But the harder Wind blew, the tighter the man wrapped his coat around himself. Finally, Wind gave up.

Sun came out from behind a cloud, shining brightly and warmly upon the man. Soon, the man was too hot. He took off his coat.

"You see," said Sun. "I am warm and kind. But you are cold and hard. Being warm and kind is a better way to get what you want."

To Be Warm and Kind

(Wind and Sun are fighting.)

SUN: I am stronger!

WIND: No, I am!

(A man comes walking down the path below.)

SUN: Let's have a test to see who is stronger. The one who makes the man take off his coat is the winner.

WIND: I will go first!

(Sun goes behind a cloud. Wind blows as hard as it can. The man holds his coat on tightly. The poor man is very cold. Soon, Wind gives up.)

(Sun comes out, smiling and shining brightly. Soon, the man gets too warm. He takes off his coat.)

WIND: You did it! You won!

SUN: That's right! You don't have to be cold and hard to get what you want. It is better to be warm and kind.

Name _____ Date _____

Respond to Reading

Read the questions. Circle the letter next to your answer.

1. The first passage is —

   a. a fable.   **b.** a play.   **c.** a biography.

2. What contest does Sun have with Wind?

   a. They try to see who can make the plants grow taller.

   b. They try to make the man take off his coat.

   c. They try to melt snow after a storm.

3. The second passage is —

   a. a poem.   **b.** a play.   **c.** a fable.

4. "To Be Warm and Kind" is a story that —

   a. uses rhythm and has many words that rhyme.

   b. tells about something that happened long ago.

   c. could be acted in front of other people.

REREAD "A Tale of the Wind and the Sun" and
"To Be Warm and Kind" on pages 81–82.

THINK about how Sun and Wind are the same and how
they are different. Use a copy of the Venn Diagram on page
152 to organize your ideas.

What is the same about how the story is told in the fable
and in the play? What is different?

_____

_____

_____

_____

_____

_____

_____

Be sure to—

1. write about what is the same and what is different.

2. use correct spelling and capitalization.

3. use your own words.

4. use correct grammar and complete sentences.

Comparing Genres • *Genre Practice*

The Fourth of July

Read the passages below. Then answer the questions that follow.

The Fourth of July is one of the best days of summer! You will see a lot of American flags. You might watch a parade or go to a party. You might eat hot dogs. There will be fireworks at night. The Fourth of July is a fun day. It is a special day. Do you know why?

The Fourth of July is a birthday party for America. Something special happened on July 4 in the summer of 1776. That was about two hundred fifty years ago. A group of men signed a paper. Back then America was not a country. The people that lived in America could not make their own laws. They had to follow the laws of another country. That country was Great Britain. The people in America did not like that. The Americans wanted to be in charge. They wanted to make their own laws.

The paper the men signed was sent to the king of Great Britain. In the paper, the people said they were not happy. They told the king they were going to be free from his laws. This paper was the Declaration of Independence. Those are big words. They mean the men declared, or said strongly, they were independent, or free from, the king's rule. America became a country!

We celebrate the history of America on every Fourth of July. On this day, we think about how the United States began. We are glad we are free.

Writing to Sources • *Genre Practice*

Respond to Reading

Read the questions. Circle the letter next to your answer.

1. This passage—

    a. is the story of someone's life.

    b. is based on facts and information.

    c. tells the reader what to think or do.

2. When did America become a country?

    a. exactly two hundred fifty years ago

    b. July 4, 1776

    c. the Fourth of July, 2018

3. What is the main idea of the passage?

    a. We remember America's history on the Fourth of July.

    b. There are parties and parades on the Fourth of July.

    c. A group of men signed a paper on July 4, 1776.

REREAD "The Fourth of July" on pages 85–86.

THINK about the facts the author gives in the passage. What are some questions about the holiday you still have? Write a list of questions. Use a copy of the Word Map graphic organizer on page 150 to organize your ideas.

How does the author describe celebrating the Fourth of July?

_____

_____

_____

_____

_____

_____

_____

_____

Be sure to—

1. use details from the passage to support your answer.

2. use your own words to retell the author's descriptions.

3. use correct spelling and capitalization.

4. use correct grammar and complete sentences.

Telling Stories

Read the passages below. Then answer the questions that follow.

It is great to have friends. It is fun to learn about their lives. How can you get to know your friends better? Ask your friends to tell you stories. They might tell stories about their lives. They might tell fun stories they make up. Telling stories is fun! Stories also help us get to know our friends better.

Learn about your friends' lives! Friends can tell you about important things that have happened. They may tell you about their families. Maybe they have a cool pet! Ask your friends about their lives. Listen to what they have to say!

Sometimes people tell made-up stories. This is a fun way to get to know a friend, too! Even made-up stories can tell you a lot. A friend may tell you a story about a wild animal. That friend may like to play outdoors. Another friend could tell you a story about a prince or princess. The story might have a happy ending. What can you find out from a story like that?

Your friends want to get to know you, too. Tell a story! You can tell your friends about real things from your life. Or you can tell a made-up story. Try telling your friends about something you like to do. Sharing stories is fun! It's also a great way to get to know your friends better.

Persuasive Text • *Genre Practice*

Respond to Reading

Read the questions. Circle the letter next to your answer.

1. This passage—

   a. is a play.

   b. gives information about fairy tales.

   c. tells what the author wants us to do.

2. What does the author think children should do?

   a. Play outdoors with friends.

   b. Tell and listen to stories with friends.

   c. Make up stories about a friend's life.

3. Which sentences best explain what this text is about?

   a. Children should tell stories to friends. It helps people get to know each other.

   b. Children should make up stories about other people. It is fun, and it will help people like each other.

   c. Children should try to talk more than their friends. Telling stories is more important than listening.

REREAD "Telling Stories" on pages 89–90.

THINK about what the author says to do. Which story would you like to tell your friends? Use the Five Ws Chart on page 149 to organize your ideas.

What kind of a story you would like to tell your friends? Why do you want to tell this story to your friends?

_____

- -

_____

- -

_____

- -

_____

- -

_____

- -

_____

Be sure to—

1. give reasons why you would tell the story to your friends.

2. use correct spelling.

3. use correct capitalization.

4. write using complete sentences.

Persuasive Text • *Genre Practice*

The Power of a Rumor

Read the passage below. Then answer the questions that follow.

Long ago, a rabbit lived in a forest. One day, the rabbit sat under a coconut tree. She began to worry. "What if the world breaks apart?"

Just then, there was a loud crash. "Oh no!" she said. "The world IS breaking apart!"

The rabbit started to run. She ran past a group of monkeys. "The world is breaking apart!" cried the rabbit.

"Oh no!" the monkeys said. The monkeys all ran after the rabbit. The rabbit and the monkeys ran as fast as they could. They passed a herd of elephants.

The last monkey to pass said, "The world is breaking apart!"

"Oh no!" the elephants said. The elephants all ran after the monkeys and the rabbit. They ran as fast as they could. Everyone ran right into a big lion.

"STOP running so fast," the lion roared. "What is the problem?"

An elephant said, "The world is breaking apart! We are running away!"

"Who started this rumor?" asked the lion.

The elephant replied, "A monkey told me."

The monkey said, "A rabbit told me."

The rabbit explained, "The world IS breaking apart. I heard a crash!"

The lion ordered the animals to stop running while he went to find the sound. He returned soon after.

"You heard a coconut fall," the lion said. "It hit a pile of rocks. The world is NOT breaking apart."

The rabbit said, "I am sorry. Next time I will be more careful. I will check the facts and not spread rumors."

Respond to Reading

Read the questions. Circle the letter next to your answer.

1. This passage —

   a. is a poem.

   b. is a folktale.

   c. is a play.

2. Who is the first to think the world is breaking apart?

   a. a rabbit   **b.** a lion   **c.** a monkey

3. What is the best summary of the passage?

   a. A rabbit sits under a coconut tree. The rabbit plays with her friends. The rabbit and her friends talk to a lion.

   b. A rabbit hears a coconut fall. She tells a monkey. The monkey tells an elephant.

   c. A rabbit thinks the world is breaking apart. She runs, and animals follow her. A lion finds out the truth.

REREAD "The Power of a Rumor" on pages 93–94.

THINK about the characters in this story. Why are the animals scared? How does the author use the scared animals to teach a lesson? Use a copy of the Story Map on page 153 to organize your ideas.

What lesson does this story teach? Use details from the passage to support your answer.

_____

_____

_____

_____

_____

_____

_____

Be sure to—

1. explain the lesson and why it is important.

2. use details from the passage to support your answer.

3. use your own words when you retell events.

4. use correct spelling and complete sentences.

Folktale • *Genre Practice*

Brave Bessie Coleman

Read the passage below. Then answer the questions that follow.

Bessie Coleman was born about one hundred twenty-five years ago. She lived in a small town in Texas. Young Bessie liked math. She was a good reader too. Bessie had a goal. She wanted to be a pilot.

To become a pilot, Bessie needed to go to flight school. But Bessie was an African American woman. At the time, flight schools would not teach African Americans. They would not teach women. Still, Bessie did not give up.

Bessie heard of schools in France that would teach her to fly. So, she learned to speak French. Then she traveled to France. A school there taught her to fly a plane. Bessie was the first African American in the world to get a pilot's license.

After flight school, Bessie flew airplanes. She was in air shows. People paid money to watch her do stunts in the air. She would sometimes jump out of the plane! She got the nickname "Brave Bessie." At the air shows, she also gave talks. She wanted other young African Americans to learn how to fly.

Bessie wanted to open a flight school for African Americans. But she died in 1926, before she could do it. Others kept her idea going. In 1929, a flight school for African Americans opened. Many African Americans learned to fly because they heard about Bessie.

In 1995, the post office made a stamp. It had Bessie Coleman's picture on it. They called her a legend.

Respond to Reading

Read each question. Circle the letter next to your answer choice.

1. This passage—

   a. is a legend.

   b. is a folktale.

   c. is a biography.

2. What is a pilot?

   a. a person who flies a plane

   b. a place where you learn to fly

   c. an airplane that can do stunts

3. What is the main idea of the passage?

   a. Bessie Coleman's picture was printed on a stamp in 1995.

   b. Bessie Coleman overcame challenges to reach her goal.

   c. Bessie Coleman had to go to France to learn to fly a plane.

REREAD "Brave Bessie Coleman" on pages 97–98.

THINK about the details the author shared about Bessie Coleman's story. How did the author organize the details? Use the Word Map on page 150 to organize your ideas.

Why do you think the author wrote this passage? Use details from the passage to support your answer.

_____

- -

_____

- -

_____

- -

_____

- -

_____

- -

_____

Be sure to—

1. tell the author's purpose for writing the passage.

2. use your own words.

3. use correct spelling, capitalization, punctuation, grammar, and complete sentences.

The Five Senses

Read the passage below. Then answer the questions that follow.

How do we know about the things around us? We see, hear, taste, touch, and smell. These are the five senses. The five senses help us learn about the world.

We see with our eyes. We can see colors, shapes, and sizes. Seeing lets us know where things are. Seeing lets us read, move around, and find things.

Our ears let us hear. Hearing is important for listening to people. It is important for learning words and for knowing what to do. Have you heard a loud fire alarm? You know just what to do when you hear it.

Touch is an important sense too. We can tell what things are because of how they feel. It is fun to feel different things. Do you like fuzzy things or smooth things best?

Our nose lets us smell. We can smell food and other scents. Smells can make us feel good. Many people like how flowers smell. Others like the smell of food.

Taste is the sense we use when we eat. We use our tongue to taste food. Some foods taste good. Other foods do not taste good. You may like a taste. Your friend may not. It is funny that the tastes we like can be so different!

Together, our five senses can help us learn almost anything. The five senses help us learn and have fun!

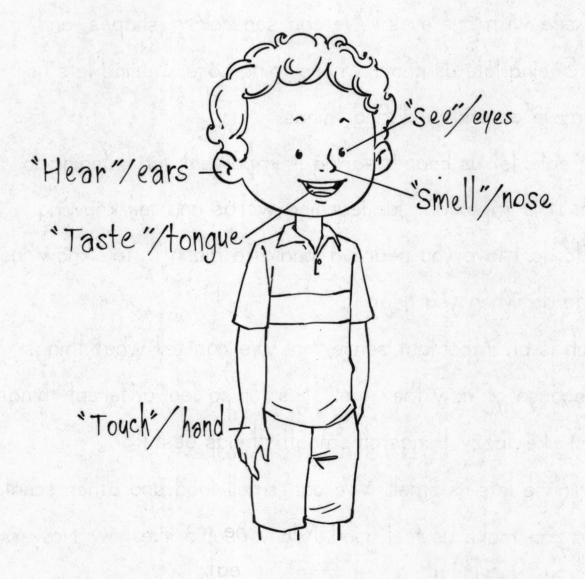

Informational Text • *Genre Practice*

Respond to Reading

Read each question. Circle the letter next to your answer choice.

1. This passage—

　　a. gives information.

　　b. tells a story.

　　c. is a folktale.

2. Why did the author put the picture on page 102?

　　a. The picture helps readers understand the five senses.

　　b. The picture shows something funny about senses.

　　c. The picture tells which of the five senses is best.

3. Which answer best explains what "The Five Senses" is about?

　　a. There are five senses. The most important is seeing. The others are not as important.

　　b. There are five senses. Each one helps people learn in different ways.

　　c. Of the five senses, tasting is the most fun. It helps us find out what foods we like to eat.

REREAD "The Five Senses" on pages 101–102.

THINK about how the author gives information in this text. How does the author tell about each sense? Use the Cluster Word Web on page 148 to organize your ideas.

How does the author help the reader learn about the five senses?

_____

_____

_____

_____

_____

_____

_____

_____

Be sure to—

1. include details from the selection.

2. use your own words.

3. use correct spelling, capitalization, punctuation, grammar, and complete sentences.

Informational Text • *Genre Practice*

What Our Humans Do Best

Read the passage below. Then answer the questions that follow.

CHARACTERS

    TIGER, an orange cat

    BELLA, a white cat

    GUS, a golden dog

    ROXIE, a brown dog

(A neighborhood park. A group of dogs and cats meet in the shade.)

ROXIE and GUS: Hello, cats!

TIGER and BELLA: Hello, dogs!

ROXIE: Hey, Gus—did you bring a ball to the park today? My human forgot mine.

GUS: *(stops chasing his tail)* I buried one here yesterday. I'll be right back.

(Gus walks behind a tree to dig up his ball.)

BELLA: *(frowning)* What's the big deal about chasing a ball around?

TIGER: Yeah, why do you two like it so much?

ROXIE: *(chewing her leg, then speaking)* It's so fun! My human throws it, and I run as fast as I can to get it.

(Gus returns and drops his ball in front of Roxie.)

GUS: And then you bring the ball back to your human, and he throws it for you again!

(Tiger and Bella trade looks.)

TIGER: I just don't get it.

ROXIE: Well, what do you cats like to do with your humans?

BELLA: Tiger and I like to cuddle with them.

TIGER: *(licking his paw)* Yes. We love when they rub our ears.

GUS: You would rather have your ears rubbed than play?

TIGER: I would rather have my ears rubbed than just about anything . . . except eating.

GUS: *(wagging his tail hard and fast)* Oh yes! I love to eat! I do like it when my human feeds me.

TIGER: Food! That's what our humans do best!

Play • *Genre Practice*

Respond to Reading

Read each question. Circle the letter next to your answer choice.

1. This passage—

   a. is a poem.

   b. is a play.

   c. is a fantasy.

2. What do Gus and Roxie tell Tiger and Bella?

   a. They tell them why it is fun to chase after a ball.

   b. They tell them how to bury toys to play with later.

   c. They tell them what kind of food they like to eat.

3. What is the main idea of the play?

   a. Cats and dogs like to talk about the things they like to do in parks.

   b. Cats and dogs can get their humans to do what they want.

   c. Cats and dogs are different in some ways, but in other ways they are the same.

REREAD "What Our Humans Do Best" on pages 105–106.

THINK about the information the author included at the beginning of the passage. Who are the characters? What is the setting? Use the Word Map on page 150 to organize your ideas.

How do you know this passage is a play? Use details from the passage to support your answer.

_____

_____

_____

_____

_____

_____

Be sure to—

1. tell about the parts of a play.

2. use your own words.

3. use correct spelling, capitalization, punctuation, grammar, and complete sentences.

The Crow and the Pitcher

Read the passage below. Then answer the questions that follow.

Many years ago, the world was very dry. There was a crow who needed water badly. In fact, he was so thirsty that he could not even fly.

The crow walked and walked. He looked for water. He had to find water or he knew he would die.

The crow saw a pitcher at the edge of a field. The pitcher might hold water. He put his head in for a drink. Sadly, there was only a little bit of water in the bottom of the pitcher. The crow almost cried. He was so thirsty, and here was a bit of water that was out of reach!

Then, the crow had an idea. He found a small rock and put it in the pitcher. The water moved up, so he put in another rock. The water moved up again. He put in lots of rocks and the water came up even more.

The rocks pushed the water up in the pitcher. At last, the water was high enough for the crow to drink. The crow dipped his beak in and drank. He felt much better. He flew away happily. That day, the crow learned a lesson. He could solve a problem by thinking hard about a solution.

Fable • *Genre Practice*

Respond to Reading

Read each question. Circle the letter next to your answer choice.

1. This passage —

   a. is a fable.

   b. is a poem.

   c. is a play.

2. What is a pitcher?

   a. something that has rocks in it

   b. something that holds water

   c. something that crows like to drink from

3. What lesson does this story teach?

   a. Keep thinking about a problem, and you can find a solution.

   b. You should look at crows to find out how to solve a problem.

   c. Putting rocks in a pitcher will raise the water up higher.

REREAD "The Crow and the Pitcher" on pages 109–110.

THINK about the beginning of "The Crow and the Pitcher." What is the crow's problem? How do you know it is a big problem? Use the Cluster Word Web on page 148 to organize your ideas.

How does the crow solve his problem at the end of the story?

_____

_____

_____

_____

_____

_____

_____

_____

_____

Be sure to—

1. include details from the passage.

2. use your own words.

3. use correct spelling, capitalization, punctuation, grammar, and complete sentences.

Fable • *Genre Practice*

The Princess and the Frog

Read the passage below. Then answer the questions that follow.

Once upon a time, there was a princess who loved to play. One day, she was playing near a pond. She threw a ball up in the air. Plop! The ball landed in the water. The ball sank, and the princess started to cry.

"Don't cry, princess," a voice croaked. The princess wiped her eyes. The princess was shocked to see a talking frog in the pond. He was holding her ball.

"I will give the ball back," the frog said. "But you must promise to let me live with you in your castle."

The princess agreed. The frog tossed the ball back to her. Then, keeping her promise, the princess scooped up the frog and took him to her castle.

It was strange at first. The frog ate from her plate and slept on her favorite pillow. But the frog also liked to play. The princess and the frog liked to tell each other stories late into the night.

One night, the princess and the frog were talking.

"You know, frog," said the princess. "You are a good friend."
And just as she said this, a magical thing happened. The frog
turned into a prince, right before her eyes! The princess
was amazed.

The prince said, "Many years ago, a witch turned me into a
frog. The spell could only be broken if a princess became my
friend. Thank you!"

The prince and princess got to know each other even better.
Soon they fell in love, and they lived happily ever after.

Respond to Reading

Read each question. Circle the letter next to your answer choice.

1. This passage—

   a. is a biography.

   b. is a fable.

   c. is a fairy tale.

2. What happens to the princess's ball?

   a. It sinks in the pond.

   b. A frog steals it.

   c. She loses it in the woods.

3. What is the story mostly about?

   a. A princess loses her ball.

   b. A princess becomes a frog's friend and breaks a spell.

   c. A princess marries a prince, and they live happily ever after.

REREAD "The Princess and the Frog" on pages 113–114.

THINK about the characters and their actions. What type of story is "The Princess and the Frog"? How do you know? Use a copy of the Story Map on page 153 to organize your ideas.

Why does the author begin the story with the words "Once upon a time"? How do these words help you understand what type of story it is?

_____

– –

_____

– –

_____

– –

_____

– –

_____

Be sure to—

1. explain why the author uses the words "Once upon a time."

2. use details from the passage to support your answer.

3. use correct spelling, capitalization, punctuation, grammar, and complete sentences.

Fairy Tale • *Genre Practice*

Nature Trails

Read both passages. Then answer the questions that follow.

Nature trails are paths through natural places. There are many kinds of trails. Some trails are short. Others are long. The Appalachian Trail is more than two thousand miles long!

Nature trails are made in different ways. A few people may get together and make a trail. Or a lot of people might make some trails. The National Park Service makes some trails as well. It takes a lot of work to make a trail.

It takes a lot of work to keep a trail open, too. Trails must be kept clear. Thousands of people work on the Appalachian Trail each year.

Nature trails let people spend time together outside. Nature trails can be found in many beautiful places.

Take a Hike

Everyone should go hiking! Hiking is a healthy activity. It is a fun way to spend time with friends. There are many kinds of trails. So find a trail that is right for you and hike it!

Hiking is good for you. Your heart is a muscle. When you hike on a hill, your heart beats harder. It gets stronger.

Taking a hike with friends is fun! Have you ever heard of a penny hike? A penny hike is a fun way to take hikes with friends. Choose two places, such as a big tree and a picnic table. Assign one place to the heads side of a penny. Assign the other to the tails side. Flip the coin to see which way to go. Then choose two new places and flip again!

Hiking is a fun and healthy activity. So take a hike!

Comparing Genres • *Genre Practice*

Respond to Reading

Read each question. Circle the letter next to your answer choice.

1. The passage "Nature Trails"—

   a. gives information.

   b. tells a story.

   c. is a biography.

2. How long is the Appalachian Trail?

   a. about two miles

   b. less than two hundred miles

   c. more than two thousend miles

3. The passage "Take a Hike"—

   a. is fiction.

   b. is persuasive text.

   c. is a play.

4. The author of "Take a Hike" says you should go hiking because —

   a. hiking with friends is fun.

   b. all cities have trails.

   c. people that hike are always busy.

5. Both "Nature Trails" and "Take a Hike"—

    a. tell a story.

    b. have facts.

    c. try to persuade readers.

6. Which passage states an opinion and uses reasons to support it?

    a. "Nature Trails"

    b. "Take a Hike"

    c. both passages

7. Which topic appears in both "Nature Trails" and "Take a Hike"?

    a. how to make a trail

    b. the reasons hiking is healthy

    c. there are many kinds of trails

8. "Nature Trails" gives facts about trails. "Take a Hike"—

    a. tells how to find hiking trails.

    b. gives different facts about trails.

    c. gives reasons why you should hike.

Name _____ **Date** _____

Comparing Genres

REREAD "Nature Trails" and "Take a Hike" on pages 117–118.

THINK about what each author wants the reader to do or to know. Use a copy of the Venn Diagram on page 152 to organize your ideas.

How are the passages alike? How are they different? Be sure to use details from the passages to support your answer.

_____

- -

_____

- -

_____

_____

_____

- -

_____

_____

- -

Revising

Use this checklist to revise your writing.

☐ Does your writing have a clear purpose?

☐ Does your writing tell how the passages are alike?

☐ Does your writing tell how the passages are different?

☐ Does your writing include details from the passages?

Editing/Proofreading

Use this checklist to correct mistakes in your writing.

☐ Did you use proofreading symbols when editing?

☐ Does your writing include transition words?

☐ Did you check for subject/verb agreement?

☐ Did you check your writing for spelling mistakes?

Publishing

Use this checklist to prepare your writing for publishing.

☐ Write or type a neat copy of your writing.

☐ Add a photograph or drawing.

More Recess!

Read the passage below. Then answer the questions that follow.

All children need time to play and move. Recess is the best time for that. Recess is a time away from schoolwork. But it is more than just a break. Recess is good for children. It helps them do better in school and stay healthy. Children learn new skills during recess. More recess makes the school day better for kids all around.

Recess helps children in many ways. Having time for free play can help children learn. Moving around at recess helps them think about what they learned in the morning. It also helps them concentrate better on schoolwork in the afternoon. A small recess makes big changes in how well children do in school. Recess helps children do better in school.

Recess also helps children stay fit. They can run around and play fun games. Being active during school makes children want to be active after school, too. Recess helps children keep their bodies healthy. Learning to be healthy now can help children for the rest of their lives.

Children also learn new skills during recess. They learn how to get along with others. They play games together. Children must take turns and share at recess. Children must learn to play fairly. They must work with friends.

Parents and teachers should give children more recess. It is more than just fun and games. Children learn while they have fun. And they have fun while they learn!

Persuasive Text • *Genre Practice*

Respond to Reading

Read each question. Circle the letter next to your answer choice.

1. This passage—

   a. tells how something works.

   b. tells the author's point of view.

   c. tells about a real person's life.

2. What is one way recess helps children with schoolwork?

   a. Recess helps children concentrate on schoolwork.

   b. Recess helps children make new friends.

   c. Recess helps children learn new games to play.

3. What does the author want schools to do?

   a. Teach more games to children at recess.

   b. Let children play inside or outside for recess.

   c. Give more recess time to children.

REREAD "More Recess!" on pages 123-124.

THINK about why the author wants children to have more recess. What reasons does the author give? Use a copy of the Cluster Word Web on page 148 to organize your ideas.

Why does the author think schools should give children more recess? Use details from the text to tell what the author says.

_____

– – – – – – – – – – – – – – – –

_____

– – – – – – – – – – – – – – – –

_____

– – – – – – – – – – – – – – – –

_____

– – – – – – – – – – – – – – – –

_____

– – – – – – – – – – – – – – – –

Be sure to —

1. tell why the author thinks children should have more recess.

2. use correct spelling.

3. use your own words.

4. use correct capitalization and punctuation.

Harriet Tubman

Read the passage below. Then answer the questions that follow.

In 1820, a brave woman was born. Her name was Harriet Tubman. Harriet Tubman was an African American. She was born enslaved. She was not free. Harriet had to work very hard. She was not allowed to go to school. She was treated very badly. Harriet very much wanted to be free.

After Harriet grew up, she escaped slavery by running away. It was very dangerous. It was against the law for enslaved people to leave their owners. It was also against the law for anyone to help enslaved people escape.

To get free, Harriet traveled on the Underground Railroad. This was not a real railroad. It was a group of people who helped enslaved people go north. As they made their way, Harriet and other runaways were taken to a new house each night. They hid during the day so they would not be caught.

Finally, Harriet was safe in the North. In most of the North, slavery was not allowed. Harriet would be safer there. But Harriet wanted to help other enslaved people escape too. After a few months, Harriet bravely went back to the South. She helped enslaved people escape using the Underground Railroad. Harriet made trip after trip, bringing more than three hundred people north where they could be free.

Harriet Tubman was a brave woman. She worked hard to help others be free. She talked to many people and made speeches. She helped change the way the United States treats people. Harriet Tubman is an American hero.

Respond to Reading

Read each question. Circle the letter next to your answer choice.

1. This passage—

   a. explains how to do something.

   b. is a poem.

   c. tells a story about a real person.

2. Why did Harriet Tubman put herself in danger by going back to the South where she could be caught?

   a. to get ideas for her speeches

   b. to help others escape slavery

   c. to visit her friends and family

3. Why does the author say that Harriet Tubman is an American hero?

   a. She helped save many people from slavery.

   b. She traveled north on the Underground Railroad.

   c. She talked to people about her life as an enslaved person.

REREAD "Harriet Tubman" on pages 127–128.

THINK about the details the author gives about Harriet Tubman. What are some reasons Harriet Tubman is an American hero? Use a copy of the Word Map on page 150 to organize your ideas.

Why do you think Harriet Tubman is an American hero?

_____

_____

_____

_____

_____

_____

_____

_____

Be sure to—

1. include facts from the story that show why Harriet Tubman is a hero.

2. use your own words.

3. use correct spelling, capitalization, punctuation, grammar, and complete sentences.

A Flower

Read the passage below. Then answer the questions that follow.

A seed goes into the ground

and out pops a sprout.

The sprout grows a stem,

and then the leaves stretch out.

The leaves reach for the sun,

and then you see a bud.

The bud becomes a flower,

and now the insects flood.

The insects pollinate the plant,

and the flower forms a seed.

Once there is a seed,

it waits for just the right breeze.

When the right air blows by,

the seed sails away on the wind.

No matter what, either near or far

the seed rides the wind, undisciplined.

If it lands near, then it arrived quickly.

If it lands far, then it traveled well.

The nearly landed seed creates a close family.

The far-traveled seed might be alone to dwell.

But no matter the distance traveled,

the seed will eventually touch earth.

It may land softly or with a thunk.

The landing itself does not determine worth.

It's the seed going into the ground

which results in dirt that is crowned.

Name _____ **Date** _____

Respond to Reading

Read each question. Circle the letter next to your answer choice.

1. This passage—

   a. is a fable.

   b. is a poem.

   c. is a fairy tale.

2. Why does the poet think a flower is a crown for the dirt?

   a. Flowers taste good.

   b. Flowers make people sneeze.

   c. Flowers are pretty.

3. What is the poem mostly about?

   a. Fish swimming in a river.

   b. A flower that grows and spreads seeds.

   c. A person talking about the weather.

REREAD "A Flower" on pages 131–132.

THINK about the poet's words and how those words make pictures in your mind. What do you see? Talk about what you see with a partner.

Write a list of the words from the poem that help you see what the poet has written. How do you feel when you picture parts of the poem?

_____

_____

_____

_____

_____

_____

_____

Be sure to—

1. think about what you see when you read the poem.

2. write all the words that help you see something.

3. tell how seeing these things makes you feel.

Community Parks

Read the passage below. Then answer the questions that follow.

Parks are a very important part of many towns. You can do lots of fun things in parks. They have interesting things to see. There is something for everyone at a park.

Parks are great places for children to play. There may be playgrounds with swings and slides. Parks may have big fields for sports like baseball and soccer. Parks may have courts for basketball. Children can play many games at parks.

Parks are good for the community as well. Sometimes people can work together on a garden in the park. They can grow food to help others. A park may have a building for other kinds of fun. People might come to hear music or see plays.

Friends and families can have picnics at parks. They can walk or ride bikes on trails. Parks with more than one trail will have a map of the trails.

Most trails will be marked differently. They will use colors or shapes to show different trails. Maps will be all over the park. When you stop to look at one, the map will tell you where you are in the park.

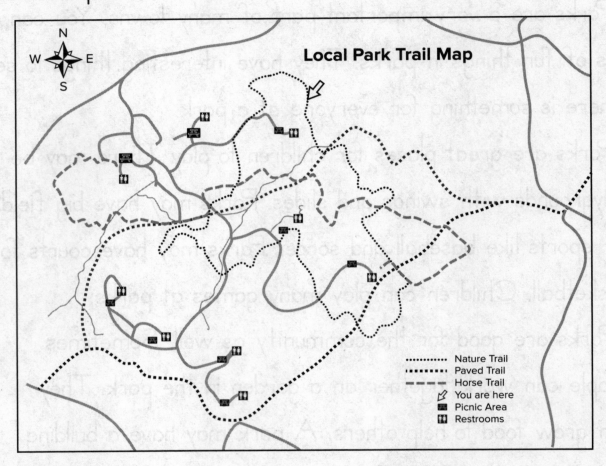

Local Park Trail Map

Nature Trail
Paved Trail
Horse Trail
You are here
Picnic Area
Restrooms

Parks are an important part of many communities. There are interesting things to see. There are fun things to do. People can rest and feel good at parks. Community parks can help people be happy and healthy.

Informational Text • *Genre Practice*

Name _____ Date _____

Respond to Reading

Read each question. Circle the letter next to your answer choice.

1. This passage—

 a. tells a story.

 b. has characters who could be real.

 c. gives facts and information.

2. Look at the map on page 136. How many kinds of trails does this park have?

 a. 3   **b.** 1   **c.** 6

3. What is the main idea of this passage?

 a. Communities must decide whether the parks will have gardens, trails, or playgrounds.

 b. Different kinds of people visit parks.

 c. Parks are important parts of communities.

REREAD "Community Parks" on pages 135–136.

THINK about the map the author put in this passage. How does the map help you understand what the park offers? Use the Four-Column Chart on page 155 to organize your ideas. Do you think the map is helpful? Explain why or why not.

_____

_____

_____

_____

_____

_____

_____

_____

_____

_____

_____

Be sure to—

1. explain why you do or do not think the map is helpful.

2. use correct spelling and capitalization.

3. use correct punctuation, grammar, and complete sentences.

Informational Text • *Genre Practice*

Name _____ Date _____

Thank You!

Read the passage below. Then answer the questions that follow.

2384 West Elm

Cooperstown, New York 13326

March 3, 2018

Dear Zoe,

Thank you for the present you sent. I am so excited to have my very own cowboy hat! Most of my friends here in New York do not have one. Now I can show them a real cowboy hat that came all the way from Arizona! You even remembered that my favorite color is red.

I love the red band on the hat. And it fits me perfectly. I want to wear it all the time! But mom says I have to take it off at the dinner table.

I am thinking of all the times I can wear my new cowboy hat. I can wear it to school on funny hat day. The other kids are sure to love it. Also, I might ask my parents if I can have a cowboy party. All the other kids can wear cowboy clothes!

Dad says we are driving to visit you and your family this summer. I will bring my cowboy hat! Do you wear one every day? Dad says you probably do not. Write back and let me know. I cannot wait to see you.

Thank you again for the great gift! I am wearing the cowboy hat now while I write this letter.

Your Cousin,

Ethan

Respond to Reading

Read each question. Circle the letter next to your answer choice.

1. This selection—

   a. is a personal letter.

   b. is a poem.

   c. is a biography.

2. Why did the author write the selection?

   a. to get the reader to buy a hat

   b. to ask his cousin a question

   c. to thank his cousin for a gift

3. What is the passage mostly about?

   a. a trip to Arizona

   b. the gift of a cowboy hat

   c. a family with cousins

Genre Practice • Personal Letter

REREAD "Thank You!" on pages 139–140.

THINK about the parts of a letter the author included. What are the five parts of a letter? Use a copy of the Word Map on page 150 to organize your ideas.

What is a gift you have received? Write a thank-you note to the person who gave you the gift.

_____

- - - - - - - - - - - - - - - - - - - -

_____

- - - - - - - - - - - - - - - - - - - -

_____

- - - - - - - - - - - - - - - - - - - -

_____

- - - - - - - - - - - - - - - - - - - -

_____

- - - - - - - - - - - - - - - - - - - -

Be sure to—

1. follow the format of a letter.

2. use correct spelling and capitalization.

3. use correct punctuation, grammar, and complete sentences.

Personal Letter • *Genre Practice*

The Friendly Dragon

Read the passage below. Then answer the questions that follow.

CHARACTERS

LI, a farmer   THE DRAGON

  CHEN, his wife   THE JADE EMPEROR

(Li and Chen are farmers in ancient China. They walk through a field.)

LI: It has not rained for weeks. Our crops are dying!

CHEN: I don't see any clouds. It won't rain today, either.

LI: The food will not grow without rain. We will starve!

BOTH: *(looking up)* Please, please rain!

(A dragon flies by. He sees the sad family, so he stops to talk.)

DRAGON: I heard you crying. What is the problem?

LI: There is no rain. Our crops are dying and my family is hungry.

DRAGON: The great Jade Emperor will know what to do. I will ask for his help. *(The dragon flies off.)*

(The Dragon enters the palace of the Jade Emperor.)

DRAGON: Mighty Jade Emperor! The farmer's family is hungry. Rain must fall so they can grow rice. Can you help?

(The Jade Emperor looks up from the game he is playing.)

JADE EMPEROR: Very well. I will help when I am done with my game.

(The Dragon flies back to Li and Chen's farm. Together, they wait for five days.)

LI: Why has the Jade Emperor not sent rain?

DRAGON: I think he has forgotten about you, but I have an idea.

(The Dragon flies to the river and sucks up all the water. He flies back to the farm and spits water out over the crops. It falls like rain.)

CHEN: We are saved! The friendly Dragon has brought the rain.

BOTH: Thank you, Dragon!

Respond to Reading

Read each question. Circle the letter next to your answer choice.

1. This passage—

   a. is about a person's life.

   b. gives information.

   c. is a play.

2. Why does the dragon decide to help the farmer?

   a. He wants to help Li and Chen.

   b. He wants to visit the Jade Emperor.

   c. He wants to play in the river.

3. What is the main idea of this story?

   a. Farmers need rain to grow crops.

   b. It is good to help people.

   c. Dragons like to help farmers.

REREAD "The Friendly Dragon" on pages 143–144.

THINK about how the author tells the story. What happens first, second, and third? Use a copy of the Story Map on page 153 to organize your ideas.

How would you describe the dragon?

_____

_____

_____

_____

_____

_____

_____

_____

Be sure to—

1. include details from the play that show what the dragon is like.

2. use your own words.

3. use correct spelling and complete sentences.

Graphic Organizer Resources

Cluster Word Web

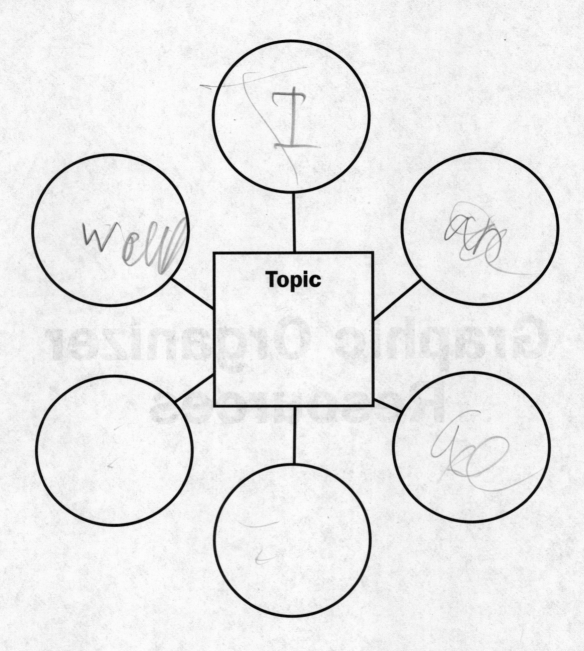

Name _____ **Date** _____

Five Ws Chart

What happened?
Who was there?
Why did it happen?
When did it happen?
Where did it happen?

Word Map

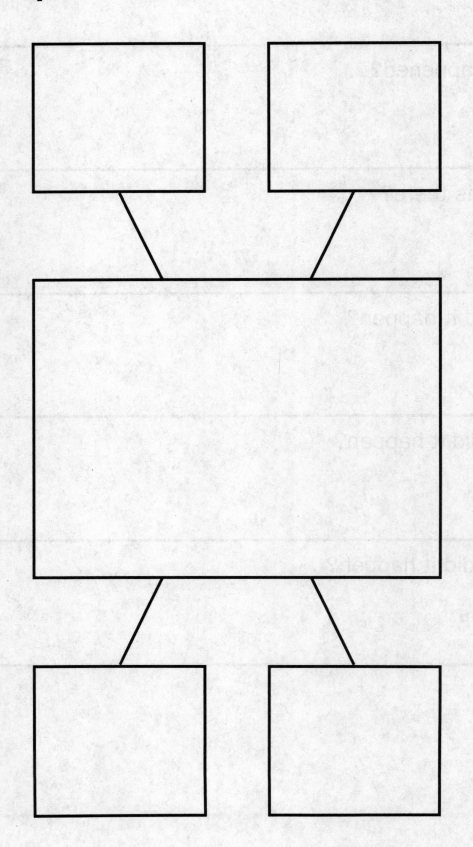

Sequence

First

Next

Last

Venn Diagram

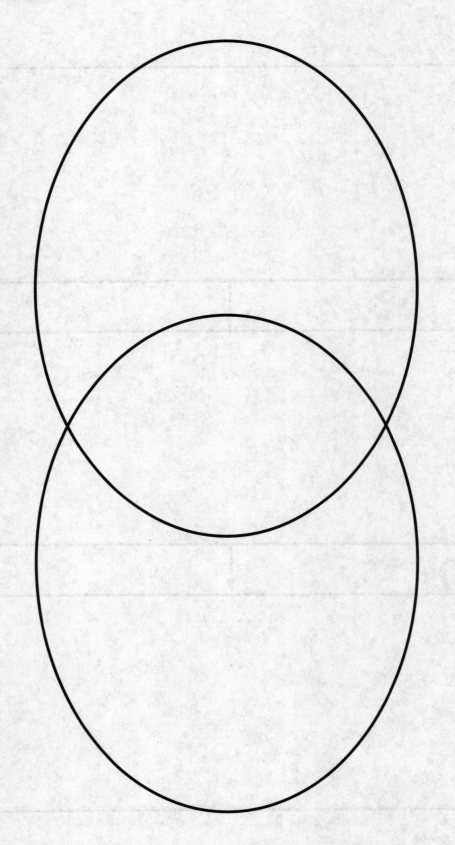

Story Map

Beginning

```



```

Middle

```



```

End

```



```

Two-Column Chart

Four-Column Chart